Catalyst

Catalyst

Poems by

Jeremy Martin

Liquid Light Press

Premium Chapbook First Edition

ISBN-10: 0988307200

ISBN-13: 978-0-9883072-0-9

Liquid Light Press

poetry that speaks to the heart

www.liquidlightpress.com

Cover Art & Design by M. D. Friedman
(*mdfriedman.com*)

Photo of Poet by Megan Martin

Dedicated to Megan

my catalyst for a better life

and to Dad

whose catalytic conversion

has already occurred.

PART I: Igniting Internal Combustion

Catalytic Converter

I want to be your secret
catalyst, quietly sparking a nuclear
reaction — nothing like a hydrogen
bomb, but more like hydrogen—

more elemental—
one nucleus, one orbit—
a simple solar system

of fusion. So let me orchestrate your atoms
until you are playing a symphony
in tune with all the submicroscopic
strings in the universe. Until you are living
this music called life.

Fossil Fuel

Words are not fossils.

The metaphorest does not harbor

flies caught in amber. Lexicons are

as alive as the skeletons

on display at your local museum, dinosauring

into your eyes, ptero-dactyling

into your ears, screeching:

You are not made

of reptiles; you are made

of angels! But beware:

Truth is part T-Rex

Terror, part Velociraptor

Rapture, rolled into one giant

saber tooth of wisdom. So open your

mouth. Let the bite of your

voice speak for you.

Petroleum Theology

The trail is littered with broken

booze bottles, a reminder of

the shattered spirits who have

trekked here before. A defunct gas

station announces: *The heart*

means everything. But the message is self-

effacing—its black graffiti

writing is on the wall

on the other side

of the road; unlike the exhaust

hogs, the heart's engine is

silent. It only revs up

when the ignition

of too many thoughts

of too many tears

is turned off.

Parenthetical Theology

I sense our nature is to be
perfected through the forge of love
(not the forgery). God is
the blacksmith; love is
the fire, and when we are pulled from
the oven—glowing and orange—He tempers
us (and our tempers) with a gentle
(but firm) mallet and anvil
into a beautiful and pleasing shape
whose true purpose
is inherent (yet maddeningly enigmatic)
in its flawless design.

A Gift of Infinite Surprise

Welcome to the furnace
of a new creation. In the pulsating center
are the dance, the dancer; the spark,
the flame. Do you dare enter?

(Of course. The universe does not place
"Do not disturb" signs on its doors.)

Fortunately, there are no fees
for your freedom, only a karmic
price: lifetimes of suffering,
in exchange for the currency of Grace.

A Brief Blaze of Grace

Enlightenment is a momentary
state of transcendence, despite what the suffering

saffron say. It is a spark of brilliance:

a mind wildfire
        a divine conflagration
                 burning the dead
                        leaves to ash.

(Save for the veins so the God blood
can flow!) Yet this moment of Grace
is only temporary, for who
can withstand the Divine

on its own terms? Yet, you are
a transformer. Be ready to unleash
your God power
into the world.

The Word Made Flash

Like molecules, words are
malleable: Turn your gold

into God! Take time to ride
the crackling current
to your heart, sail
its red rivers, voyage
using parsecs   not miles.

Surf that EKG wave
shooting through your tachyon
heart. Gaze in amazement
while it lassos
its quantum connections.

(So much for gravity

                    and greeting cards!)

Best if you surrender
to its juice. Best if you drink
its voltage, let it shock
you into arrest.

At Home in the Moment

The best happiness comes unbidden

like a gift of grace

after clouds of doubt

like a sunny afternoon

after morning storm

like halogen poems

after power outages

like a new lover never leaving

even after all your bulbs

have long since burned out.

You see, joy, like love,

needs no reason to emerge.

It sprouts of its own accord.

The rational quicksand of your gray matter

transforms into fertile soil for dendrites

to shoot and launch

into the sky, where their nuclei

seize the sun to its core.

No Analogy Seems Adequate

Love is the rocket

fuel to propel you fast enough

to break the grip of your earth

mind and its beloved

gravity. Love is an antimatter

explosion to annihilate

your fear, catapult

your faith beyond the light

barrier. Love is a nuclear

bomb to mushroom

cloud your consciousness

into inner space.

Discover your micro-cosmos as

Infinite

Beautiful

Dangerous!

From solar systems

to electron orbits

bounce from one

force to another

until you surf subatomic

seas, imploding

into your own black hole

of perfect release.

Rest Stop

Your internal universe knows
no horizon
no dimension; it is
infinite and infinitesimal—

A cell is a planet; an atom orbits
like a solar system; a hurricane spins

like a galaxy. Each universe floats
as a cell in the body of God.

He is always swimming,
all-ways admiring you
in the reflection pool.

Dive in to the divine! You and God
are helixed into an eternal
dance that never ends.

Yes, life is a paradox.

But that's paradise for the spirit.

Far better to find the rest

stop within your own resistance.

Far better to embrace this mystery

and let go of all your ill-usions.

Far better to surrender

to your inner hurricane

and let the omniscient eye

carry you home.

Gaze through your third eye

at your internal universe—

It is Beautiful

                    Infinite

                              Dangerous.

From solar systems

to electron orbits,

bounce from one

force to another

until you surf subatomic

seas, imploding

into your own black hole

of perfect release.

PART II: Riding the Zeitgeist Lightning

Breaking the Sound Barrier

Dear friends, if you cannot handle
my lightning, then go back to
the thunder and pillow
your reserves there. If you want
enlightenment, sound is not
the way to go. Your aviation must be
supersonic, your hearing
ultrasonic, if you hope to distance
yourself from the cacophony of all
your internal barriers, imploding
in marvelous, unplanned
demolition.

Inspiration

The mind is a tool for reaching, the heart
a field for receiving, and in between branches out
the lungs—inhaling
paradise—exhaling
paradox—as the cycle of
cosmic (and comic) respiration
continues.

The Eternal Playground

Dear Traveler, for that journey from the head

to the heart, not even light

can traverse, but I suppose that's what the universe

is for—a campground of eternal play, a game

where the object is to find something

you never lost. The Garden of Eden

has never abandoned us, nor

have we ever departed. But

oh how we love to create

Hell in our own fashion, as a denial of

the Heaven within.

The Infernal Racket

You are your own Big

Bang! (Though you should sing
this secret silently to yourself) for when people hear

of its resplendent resonance (Northern Lights
eat your green heart out) they tend to

get fired up from the inside
out, till Hell becomes a momentary

blessing, instead of an infinite
curse.

Parsec Parlor Trick

                                              Abandoned

                                                      in

                                                    your

                                              embrace

strange (and estranged)

how this

                                                  orgasm
is now

                                              a chasm

between us

propelling me

like a rocketship in reverse

hurt-ling me

heartlong

through my vast

inner universe

as a disconsolate amoeba

disintegrating

through the vacuum   of deep space

my protoplasm jettisoning

spinning off its axis

flicking my purposeless atoms

into star receptacles

whose light merely reflects   an illusion

An Aria for Love

Sun breaks over the emerald cliffs
for another day. No happiness
but this. A simple life.

Our morning ritual: You comb
my hair; I run my fingers through
yours. This easy intimacy
I relish. Your kiss
grounds me before I fly
away again. Instead of soaring
over the cliffs, I fly
into your embrace as you bulls eye
my heart. A target
you always hit, the mark
I unveil to you willingly.

Watch as the arc of the universe
bends toward our love. Your arrow
quills into my pupils, and I am
mesmerized by the nebulae
in your irises. Once again, I capsize
in your eyes. At night we gaze
at the neon green aurora reflecting
our magnetism, dancing
in our field of vision. We move
to its subtle, enigmatic music.

Stars—billions of stars—
spin around us. Celestial—Celeste—
one who sings in tune
with the constellations—fill me up
with your light. I cannot wait
till sunrise.

Playing the Conundrum at Elysium Hall

Paradise is rising within
you, giving birth to
new moons, ready to eclipse your
ecstasy. For you must understand
paradise is mute. You talk
to Her, she listens. Your words
are an island, Her ears

the receptive sea. But oh, how her waves are
garrulous! They love out loud
as they shout: *Swim*
into your Elemental Self. Then, dive deeper!
Join the paradise peep show. Watch Her
roll inward toward infinite
dimensions—an orgasmic origami
on a God scale—implosions exploding

into space. She's a Chinese finger trap siphoned
from your brain! So go ahead and take off
your serpentine mask. Look beyond
your eyes to see Her fathomless
face, galaxies in the black holes of Her dilated
pupils, and on the other side of Her
visage, the convex mirror to perplex your
convoluted cortex, to flex your
myocardium into permanent contraction.

The Prism Schism

Inside each of us
is an Inner Garden
of Eden before the Fall,
but after we had already fallen

in love with life. In this magical place
tree roots are woven of liquid
gold, flowing with the garnet, sparkling
rivers, winding into the fuchsia fusion
of a distant, vermillion star. Branches
unfurl diamond leaves, flowering
orange and yellow through their facets, veining
from fingers of green and indigo, reaching
out to the jade and sapphire blades

of grass below. In this miraculous place

you and your lover are One, and when

you choose to separate, you connect

to the life pulsating

all around you. In that sacred moment

you and God build a monument

impervious to rust. You are

on holiday, on any continent

vast enough to form volcanic

oceans, cracking open this ice

of existence, sliding down the fissure

toward the benevolent radiation

into your molten core. It is time to enter

that aviary where all colors are flying

white pyramids, their spectral

universe parading

in beguiling disguise.

Amazement

Use your anagrammatic magic
to discover the EDEN within

NEED. But don't go all in
on paradise yet. You might roll
snake eyes, tempt that old
serpent to slither into the labyrinth
inside your ear, its forked tongue coiling
in your cochlea, hissing:
I am the apple
of your third eye. The branches
of the trees of knowledge and life helix
through your vertebrae, ascend
beyond their 33 spinal stations, accelerate
at a pace that turns light
into snail DNA. You must slow down
long enough to witness
infinity, bending
on one knee, proposing
marital bliss.

Time to Get Out of the Gene Pool

You must stop thinking
in helixes and atoms. Instead, you should start
sensing that Love animates us

                        guides us

             sustains us

   and yes

                           even sings

us. For when we are in tune with
God's will, we are symphonies of
euphonious sound and mesmerizing light.

Life then transforms into eternal rivers,
flowing into nuclear
sunsets, ascending ornamental
staircases

into a cloudless horizon. Follow me
people of the flesh, beings
of the spirit. Your true mansion
awaits.

Graduation Day

Flip your dogma over, let it
roll over and play
dead. This canine is
amgod now. It's a whole new
game to consider.

For you have always known

you are more
divine than doctrine
more dharma than drama
more deity than piety.

It's time to stop
denying
your True Self. Fly into
the God within! The sky is
no longer

the limit. That cindering cerulean, those siphoning

suns are only the burning

stages of jettisoned booster rockets

as you climb

toward new dimensions

of dazzling, never-

ending commencement ceremonies.

About the Author

Jeremy A. Martin was born in Hershey, Pennsylvania, and lived in nearby Palmyra until he was eighteen. After graduating from high school, he moved to Galesburg, Illinois, to attend Knox College for his BA in English. He then continued his studies at Eastern Washington University in Spokane, Washington, to receive his MFA in creative writing. He now lives with his wife, Megan, in Flagstaff, Arizona, where he has been teaching composition and creative writing at Coconino Community College for the last four years. His hobbies include reading, hiking, and traveling as well as listening to and mixing music. He is currently working on his first novel and a second book of poems. *Catalyst*, his first book, was inspired by a dream that told him it was time to reawaken his passion for writing and to share that passion with others.

Other Books from Liquid Light Press

Leaning Toward Whole, Poems by M. D. Friedman
(Released June, 2011)

This poetry chapbook from the international award winning poet, M. D. Friedman, contains pieces both poignant and personal. *Leaning Toward Whole* speaks to both the universal and the everyday, both the moment and the millennium.

The Miracle Already Happening - Everyday Life with Rumi,
Poems by Rosemerry Wahtola Trommer
(Released December, 2011)

Rosemerry Wahtola Trommer's superb collection of poems, inspired by Rumi, is full of heart, humor, peace and wisdom. This chapbook gracefully flings us from our routine into the joy of life, bristles with surprise and dances with mystic vision.

Spiral, Poems by Lynda La Rocca
(Released March, 2012)

Award winning poet, Lynda La Rocca, creates a compelling poetic and melodic discourse from the persistent cravings and fears inside of each of us. This book is both as darkly sweet and satisfying as chocolate and as nourishing and healing as mother's chicken soup.

From the Ashes, Poems by Wayne A. Gilbert
(Released June , 2012)

Master jazz Sufi poet, Wayne A. Gilbert, chronicles the loss of his mother with powerful, bittersweet honesty to create this beautiful collection of poems that is universal in its scope, transcendent in the depth of its understanding and exquisitely musical in form.

ah, Poems by Rachel Kellum'
(Released July, 2012)

Rachel Kellum's first published book is a transparent poetic odyssey into the ethereal that is both provocative and inspirational. With ah Rachel Kellum demonstrates a maturity of craft that bespeaks the power of poetry to suggest what logic always struggles to explain about our divine nature.

All Liquid Light Press books are available directly from *www.liquidlightpress.com* both in print and as e-books or from any of the current major global distribution channels including Amazon, Barnes and Noble, the iBookstore and the Ingram Catalog.